TECHNIQUE OF THE
SAXOPHONE

Rhythm Studies

Joseph Viola

VOLUME 3

Berklee Press

Director: Dave Kusek
Managing Editor: Debbie Cavalier
Marketing Manager: Ola Frank
Sr. Writer/Editor: Jonathan Feist

ISBN 0-7935-5428-4

1140 Boylston Street
Boston, MA 02215-3693 USA
(617) 747-2146

Visit Berklee Press Online at
www.berkleepress.com

DISTRIBUTED BY

HAL•LEONARD®
CORPORATION
7777 W. BLUEMOUND RD. P.O. BOX 13819
MILWAUKEE, WISCONSIN 53213

Visit Hal Leonard Online at
www.halleonard.com

THE TECHNIQUE OF THE SAXOPHONE

PART III

RHYTHM STUDIES FOR SAXOPHONE

Introduction

"Rhythm Studies for Saxophone" is designed to provide the interme-
diate or advanced saxophonist with comprehensive reading experience
in a variety of rhythmic styles and notational systems. The method
is divided into four sections and the following outline should assist
the student in establishing an effective practice routine for each
section.

Section I

The main purpose of the material is to provide rhythmic reading
experience in simple time signatures. The notation is often delib-
erately complex and will familiarize the player with unconventional
but often used forms of rhythmic notation as he acquires skill in
reading syncopated rhythmic passages. The short duets illustrating
the comparitive notations used in $\frac{4}{4}$ and $\frac{2}{2}$ are important. The "A"
and "B" portions of each example are the same. Only the notational
system is different. Any comfortable tempo is acceptable and con-
tinued repetition of both parts of the duet is essential. Examples
in $\frac{12}{8}$ are to be played with the same interpretation as the related
$\frac{4}{4}$ examples.

> Note: Only three types of articulation are used
> throughout the book:

$$— = \text{long}$$

$$\wedge = \text{short}$$

$$> = \text{normal accent}$$

All other decisions regarding articulation and expression are at the
discretion of the player.

Section II

This section begins with a series of short examples in a variety of
simple and compound time signatures. Repeat each example until you
are able to play it comfortably and gradually increase speed until
you are able to read and interpret each example at any reasonable
tempo. The extended etudes following these introductory exercises
provide reading experience in varying time signatures. Do not be
intimidated by the frequent time signature changes. Count each bar
but work toward feeling the "flow" of the music.

Section III

These are "double-time" exercises in a variety of time signatures and you may initially find it necessary to work on isolated bars or phrases at very slow tempos. In Examples 1 through 6, note that the last two bars of each example are identical to the first four bars; only the pulse changes. In bars 1 through 4, count 4 to the bar; in bars 5 and 6, count 2 to the bar.

The concluding extended exercises and etudes incorporate characteristic double time patterns. Again, each should be approached in a <u>musical</u> fashion and the double-time sections should be felt on an <u>integral</u> part of the compositional form.

Section IV

These concluding advanced etudes incorporate application of all of the rhythmic concepts developed in previous sections. In Etudes 12 through 15, a new concept is introduced and the following clarification may be helpful. After establishing the indicated metronome setting, simply remember that each bar occupies one metronome division, ie. a bar of $\frac{5}{4}$ occupies the same clock time duration as a bar of $\frac{3}{4}$ (or $\frac{4}{4}$ or $\frac{7}{4}$ etc.)

Remember throughout the book that an awareness of both rhythmic notation and rhythmic interpretation are essential in developing reading skills. Interpretation is always at the discretion of the player and/or instructor and all exercises and etudes may (and should) be played in a variety of styles.

Joseph Viola

TABLE OF CONTENTS

SECTION I

1A

1B

2A

2B

1

3A

3B

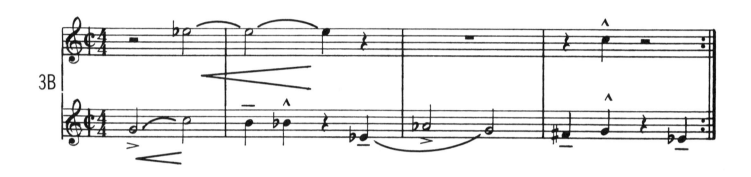

4A

4B

5A

5B

6A

6B

7A

7B

8A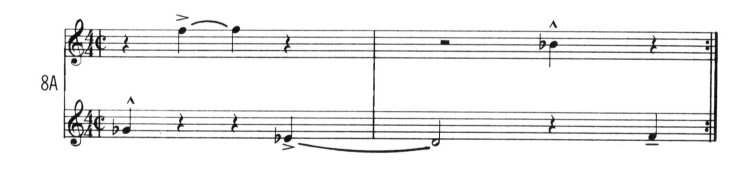

8B

5

13A

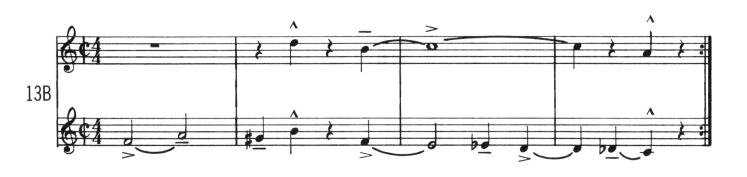

13B

14A

14B

15A

15B

16A

16B

17A

17B

18A

18B

9

19A

19B

20A

20B

22A

22B

23A

23B

26A

26B

27A

27B

17

28A

28B

18

30A

30B

31A

31B

21

32A

32B

22

34A

34B

24

35A

35B

25

36A

36B

37A

37B

27

38A

38B

28

39A

39B

29

40A

40B

41A

41B

31

42A

42B

43A

43B

44A

44B

34

45A

45B

35

46A

46B

36

47A

47B

37

48A

48B

49A

49B

51

SECTION II

18

19

20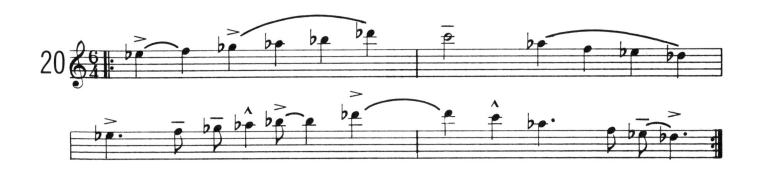

21

67

36

40

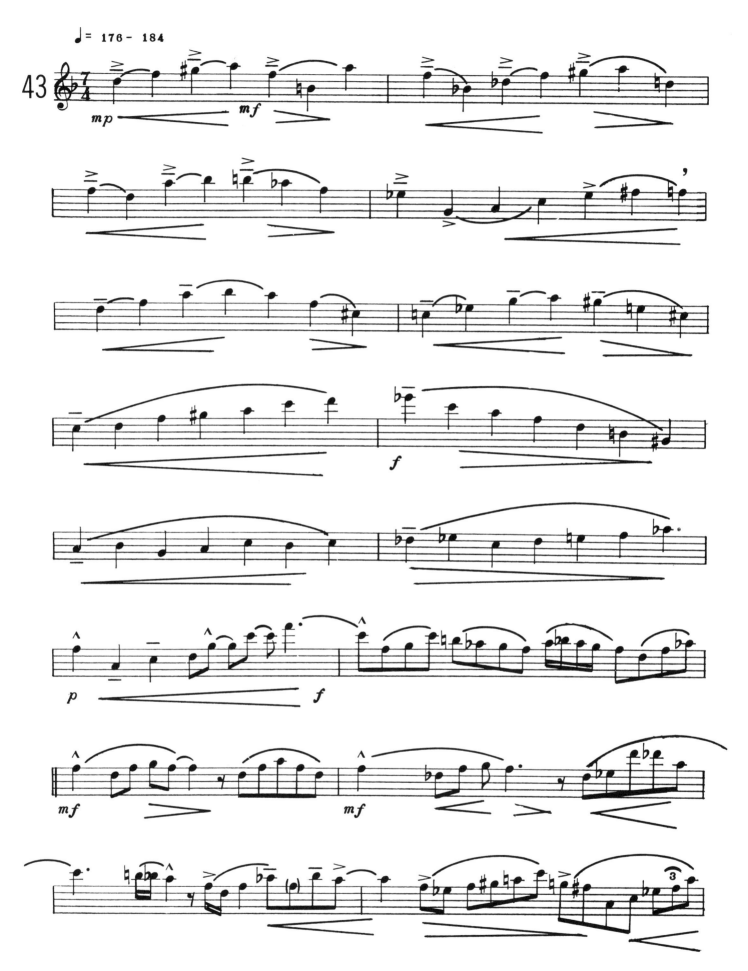

SECTION III

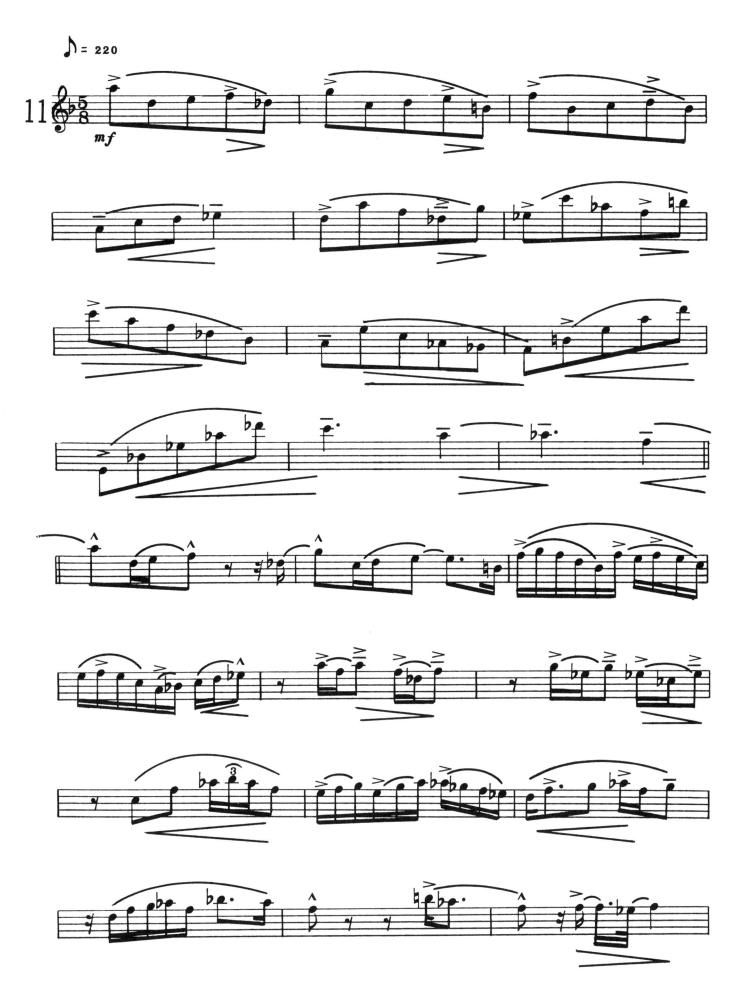

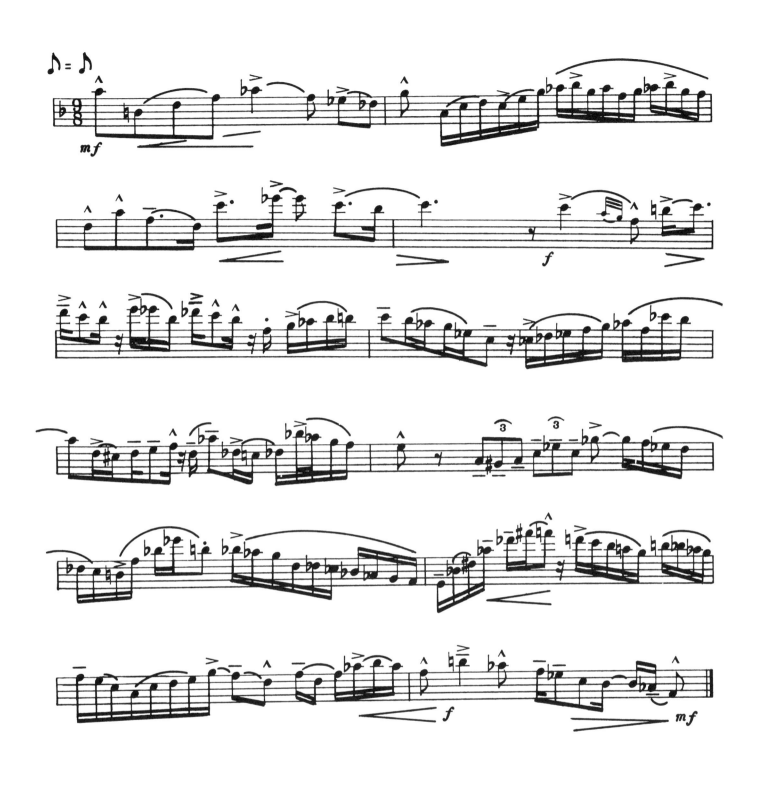

slightly faster

Tempo I

SECTION IV

ETUDE NO. 1

95

ETUDE NO. 2

V.S.

97

98

ETUDE NO. 3

ETUDE NO. 4

ETUDE NO. 5

ETUDE NO. 6

V.S.

104

ETUDE NO. 7

ETUDE NO. 7

V.S.

ETUDE NO. 8

111

ETUDE NO. 9

ETUDE NO. 10

115

ETUDE NO. 11

ETUDE NO. 12

each bar = 66 M.M.

ETUDE NO. 13

each bar = 60 to 72 M.M.

119

ETUDE NO. 14

each bar = 76 to 82 M.M.

ETUDE NO. 15

ETUDE NO. 15

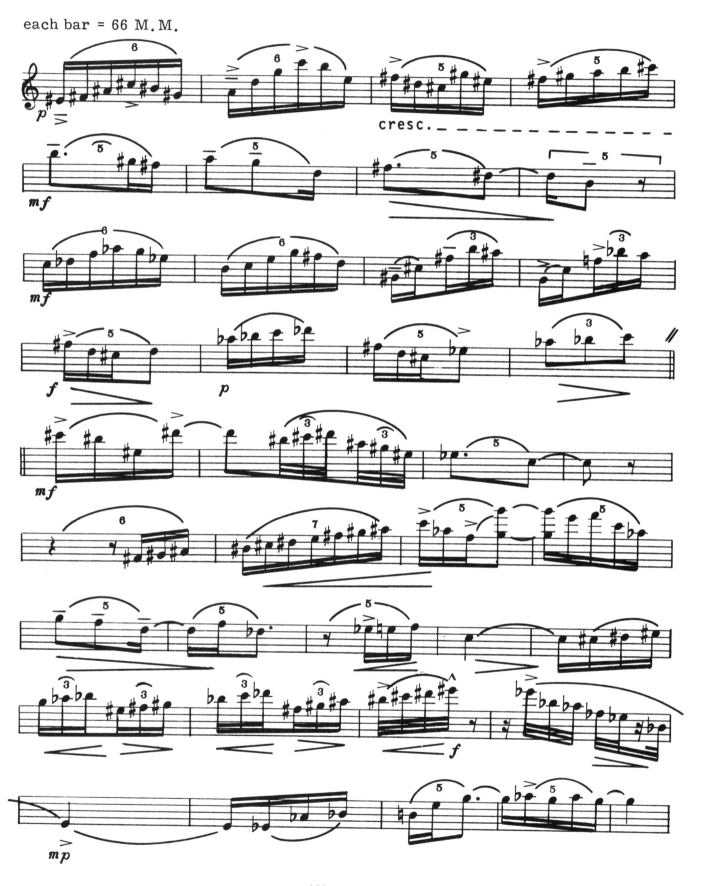

each bar = 66 M.M.

Plug into the latest technology

with
Berklee Press

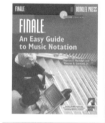

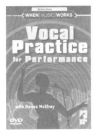

Check out more titles from Berklee Press

As Serious About Music As You Are.

SAXOPHONE

Creative Reading Studies for Saxophone
by Joseph Viola
50449870 Book $14.95
ISBN: 0-634-01334-3

Technique of the Saxophone
by Joseph Viola
50449820 **Volume 1: Scale Studies** $14.95
ISBN: 0-7935-5409-8
50449830 **Volume 2: Chord Studies** $14.95
ISBN: 0-7935-5412-8
50449840 **Volume 3: Rhythm Studies** ... $14.95
ISBN: 0-7935-5428-4

TOOLS FOR DJS

Turntable Technique: The Art of the DJ
by Stephen Webber
50449482 Book/2-Record Set $34.95
ISBN: 0-87639-010-6

Turntable Basics by Stephen Webber
50449514 Book $9.95
ISBN: 0-634-02612-7

BERKLEE PRACTICE METHOD

Get Your Band Together
Bass by Rich Appleman and John Repucci
50449427 Book/CD $14.95
ISBN: 0-634-00650-9
Drum Set by Ron Savage and Casey Scheuerell
50449429 Book/CD $14.95
ISBN: 0-634-00652-5
Guitar by Larry Baione
50449426 Book/CD $14.95
ISBN: 0-634-00649-5
Keyboard by Russell Hoffmann and Paul Schmeling
50449428 Book/CD $14.95
ISBN: 0-634-00651-7
Alto Sax by Jim Odgren and Bill Pierce
50449437 Book/CD $14.95
ISBN: 0-634-00795-5
Tenor Sax by Jim Odgren and Bill Pierce
50449431 Book/CD $14.95
ISBN: 0-634-00789-0
Trombone by Jeff Galindo
50449433 Book/CD $14.95
ISBN: 0-634-00791-2
Trumpet by Tiger Okoshi and Charles Lewis
50449432 Book/CD $14.95
ISBN: 0-634-00790-4
Vibraphone by Ed Saindon
50449438 Book/CD $14.95
ISBN: 0-634-00794-7
Violin by Matt Glaser and Mimi Rabson
50449434 Book/CD $14.95
ISBN: 0-634-00792-0

BERKLEE INSTANT SERIES

Bass by Danny Morris
50449502 Book/CD $14.95
ISBN: 0-634-01667-9
Drum Set by Ron Savage
50449513 Book/CD $14.95
ISBN: 0-634-02602-X
Guitar by Tomo Fujita
50449522 Book/CD $14.95
ISBN: 0-634-02951-7
Keyboard by Paul Schmeling and Dave Limina
50449525 Book/CD
ISBN: 0-634-03141-4

IMPROVISATION SERIES

Blues Improvisation Complete
by Jeff Harrington
Book/CD
50449486 **Bb Instruments** $19.95
ISBN: 0-634-01530-3
50449488 **C Bass Instruments** $19.95
ISBN: 0-634-01532-X

50449425 **C Treble Instruments** $19.95
ISBN: 0-634-00647-9
50449487 **Eb Instruments** $19.95
ISBN: 0-634-01531-7

A Guide to Jazz Improvisation
by John LaPorta
Book/CD
50449439 **C Instruments** $16.95
ISBN: 0-634-00700-9
50449441 **Bb Instruments** $16.95
ISBN: 0-634-00762-9
50449442 **Eb Instruments** $16.95
ISBN: 0-634-00763-7
50449443 **Bass Clef** $16.95
ISBN: 0-634-00764-5

MUSIC TECHNOLOGY

Arranging in the Digital World
by Corey Allen
50449415 Book/GM disk $19.95
ISBN: 0-634-00634-7

Finale: An Easy Guide to Music Notation
by Thomas E. Rudolph and
Vincent A. Leonard, Jr.
50449501 Book/CD-ROM $59.95
ISBN: 0-634-01666-0

**Producing in the Home Studio with Pro
Tools Second Edition** by David Franz
50449526 Book/CD-ROM $34.95
ISBN: 0-87639-008-4

Recording in the Digital World
by Thomas E. Rudolph and
Vincent A. Leonard, Jr.
50449472 Book $29.95
ISBN: 0-634-01324-6

MUSIC BUSINESS

**How to Get a Job in the Music & Recording
Industry** by Keith Hatschek
50449505 Book $24.95
ISBN: 0-634-01868-X

**Mix Masters: Platinum Engineers Reveal
Their Secrets** by Maureen Droney
50448023 Book $24.95
ISBN: 0-87639-019-X

The Musician's Internet by Peter Spellman
50449527 Book $24.95
ISBN: 0-634-03586-X

**The New Music Therapist's Handbook,
Second Edition** by Suzanne B. Hanser
50449424 Book $29.95
ISBN: 0-634-00645-2

The Self-Promoting Musician
by Peter Spellman
50449423 Book $24.95
ISBN: 0-634-00644-4

POP CULTURE

Inside the Hits by Wayne Wadhams
50449476 Book $29.95
ISBN: 0-34-01430-7

**Masters of Music: Conversations with
Berklee Greats**
by Mark Small and Andrew Taylor
50449422 Book $24.95
ISBN: 0-634-00642-8

ARRANGING

Arranging for Large Jazz Ensemble
by Ken Pullig and Dick Lowell
50449528 Book/CD $39.95
ISBN: 0-634-03656-4

Modern Jazz Voicings
by Ted Pease and Ken Pullig
50449485 Book/CD $24.95
ISBN: 0-634-01443-9

Reharmonization Techniques by Randy Felts
50449496 Book $29.95
ISBN: 0-634-01585-0

SONGWRITING / VOICE

Complete Guide to Film Scoring
by Richard Davis
50449417 Book $24.95
ISBN: 0-634-00636-3

The Contemporary Singer by Anne Peckham
50449438 Book/CD $24.95
ISBN: 0-634-00797-1

Essential Ear Training by Steve Prosser
50449421 Book $14.95
ISBN: 0-634-00640-1

Melody in Songwriting by Jack Perricone
50449419 Book $19.95
ISBN: 0-634-00638-X

Music Notation by Mark McGrain
50449399 Book $19.95
ISBN: 0-7935-0847-9

The Songs of John Lennon by John Stevens
50449504 Book $24.95
ISBN: 0-634-01795-0

The Songwriter's Workshop: Melody
by Jimmy Kachulis
50449518 Book $24.95
ISBN: 0-634-02659-3

**Songwriting: Essential Guide to Lyric Form
and Structure** by Pat Pattison
50481582 Book $14.95
ISBN: 0-7935-1180-1

Songwriting: Essential Guide to Rhyming
by Pat Pattison
50481583 Book $14.95
ISBN: 0-7935-1181-X

DISTRIBUTED BY

HAL•LEONARD®